Manners
In America

Are Dead

95 Quick & Powerful Tips To Win People Over
with the Power of Politeness

SONYA CHAPMAN

Copyright © 2018, Sonya Chapman.

All rights reserved.

No part of this book may be reproduced or transmitted in any form or by any means, electronic or mechanical, including photocopying, recording, or by any information retrieval system, without permission in writing from the publisher.

Writing & Publishing Process by PlugAndPlayPublishing.com
Book Cover by Tracey Miller TraceOfStyle.com
Edited by Jenny Butterfield

ISBN-10: 1986306151
ISBN-13: 978-1986306157

Disclaimer: This book contains opinions, ideas, and experiences. The purchaser and/or reader of these materials assumes all responsibility for the use of this information. Sonya Chapman and Publisher assume no responsibility and/or liability whatsoever for any purchaser and/or reader of these materials.

This book is dedicated to my parents, Louis and Sarah Carter. Thanks for teaching me manners and everything I've put into this book. Thanks for being my inspiration.

Miss you, daddy! You always believed in me.

RIP Louis Carter: 1936-2015.

To my husband, Bennie, and children, Benjamin and Erin: you all make life easy. Words could never express my love and appreciation.

Table of Contents

Read This First 1

You Can Catch More Flies with 5
Honey Than Vinegar

Two Ears, One Mouth 11

You Are Their First Teacher 17

Don't Do THAT! 21

Speak Up and Say Something 29

Oops! I Hope I Didn't Say the 33
Wrong Thing

Don't Invade Someone's Personal 43
Boundaries

People with a Disability Want to Be 47
Treated Like Everyone Else

Respect Your Elders 51

How to Stay Friends Forever 53

Be A Gracious Guest 61

High Touch Always Beats High Tech 65

The Bare Essentials to Dining Out 73

Your Next Steps… 81

About the Author 83

Book Sonya Chapman For Your Next Event! 85

Read This First

At some point in the last 40 years, American life changed. Families used to eat dinner together, play board games together, and watch their favorite TV shows together. However, in today's technology-driven, always-on-the-go society, most American families have changed how they spend time together and how they communicate with others.

Instead of enjoying dinner together at the table, where we learned about each other's day, likes and dislikes, and how to treat one another, we now typically eat on the run. Instead of laughing and bonding while playing board games together, we now entertain ourselves with our mobile devices, most times in solitude. And instead of watching our favorite TV shows together, where we could bond over the characters or enjoy a laugh together, we now live separate lives in separate rooms watching videos or playing games with "friends" from all over the world.

Honestly, when I think about the way most American family members live separate lives from each other, I feel sad. We're losing the connections our families once had, and we're losing the ability to communicate.

This sad shift in American family life is why I fear manners in America are dead. Trust, respect, and communication skills used to be taught in the home. Families used to value their relationships and always offered a helping hand when needed. I grew up in the days when my mom "embraced her village" (which consisted of extended family members, friends, neighbors, and teachers), and if I didn't respect an adult, I had an army of people who would be disappointed with my actions.

Nowadays things are different, and this difference is why I wrote this book. This book is not about being stuffy or giving you rules to follow. There are plenty of books today that serve that purpose. Instead, this book is about simple ways to treat people and about the role that politeness plays in our everyday interactions with family members, friends, neighbors, and co-workers.

Inside the following pages, you'll discover 13 easy-to-read chapters with 95 easy-to-follow tips on how you can be courteous and make others around you feel respected, appreciated, and comfortable in any situation.

Don't let this book's simple presentation fool you. Manners are not just about rules or actions. Manners are about your attitude toward yourself and others. This book will help you treat yourself better and help you treat others with more respect and kindness. And in turn, the tips you learn in this book will help you go further in life. Judge Clarence Thomas says it best: "Good manners will open doors the best education can't."

You Can Catch More Flies with Honey Than Vinegar

When I was a little girl, my mom would often say, "You can catch more flies with honey than vinegar."

As a little girl who didn't like insects or bugs, this saying confused me. After all, I didn't want to catch flies. I wanted them to go somewhere else.

However, I was curious. Why would I want to catch flies? So, I asked my mother what she meant. She replied, "Honey is sweet, and vinegar is sour. No one wants to be around a bunch of sour people."

Oh! Now that made sense. She wasn't talking about real flies. She was talking about making friends and being nice to people.

Being nice isn't hard to do, and being nice doesn't cost you anything. In fact, being nice can help you gain many perks in life. For example, my daughter and I were at a fast food restaurant recently, and we were discussing how rude some of the people in line were. As we approached the register to order our food, the worker appeared very irritated and frustrated. Instead of letting her mood and energy irritate me, I simply placed my order using my politeness power phrases: may I, please, and thank you. I also watched my tone and smiled.

Would you care to guess how she reacted? Of course. Her demeanor completely changed. She went from having a frown on her face to smiling. She even complimented me on my necklace.

Why did this happen? Because I was nice. Look, when you're nice to people, they tend to be nice back to you.

Here's something else interesting about that story: the place was very busy, and my daughter and I had to wait for an extra seven minutes for our food. While others made a stink about the wait, we stood there patiently with smiles on our faces. After all, the situation wasn't the cashiers fault,

and we weren't about to let this minor
ience ruin our day.

Do you know what happened next? Kay, the-once
-frowning-now-smiling cashier, offered us a light
desert for free because we had to wait. Do you
think anyone else was offered a free dessert? Not
a one.

Now, I don't know the real reason we received a
free dessert, but I would like to think the free gift
had a lot to do with being nice to Kay and treating
her kindly.

Remember, being nice is not only the right thing
to do, being nice is easy and can make a difference
in other people's lives.

Here are some tips to help you become nicer and
more pleasant to be around:

Use Affirmations

Start telling yourself every day, "This is going to
be a great day for me, I choose to be NICE today."
Listen, being nice starts from the inside. When
you're nice to yourself and you feel good about

yourself, you'll start to naturally treat other people better.

Smile and Keep a Pleasant Look on Your Face

Smiling is a sign of friendship and trust. When you smile and look pleasant, you become more approachable.

Think of Other People's Feelings

Sometimes, we are so full of ourselves that we fail to think about those around us. Showing empathy to those around us can change their world and yours. When communicating with someone, try to put yourself in her shoes. Try to feel how she feel. This simple act will allow you to see where she's coming from and see what she truly need – for you to be nice.

Be Considerate and Respect Others

You may be smarter or more aware of what's going on in the world, but that doesn't give you the right to treat anyone poorly or in a disrespectful manner. The core principles of good manners are being considerate, respectful, and tactful. Plus, being respectful and considerate is contagious. When you're considerate and respectful, others will show you the same respect and consideration.

Watch Your Tone and Language

Have you ever heard the phrase, "It's not what you say but how you say it?" The way you say something – your tone – can either brighten someone's day or hurt her feeling. Avoid having a harsh or sarcastic tone in your voice. In addition, watch your language around those you don't know and do not swear. Language is a powerful tool. Your language and your tone say a lot about you. You never want to give a person the wrong impression of who you are.

Sonya Chapman

Two Ears, One Mouth

My mom used to tell me, "You have two ears and one mouth for a reason. Try to use them as God intended, and listen more than you speak."

Listening gives you clues on what to say and what not to say. If all you're doing is talking, then you cannot possibly know or understand what your family member, friend, boss, or co-worker is trying to communicate. And if you don't know what they're trying to communicate, then you cannot respond in an appropriate way.

Have you ever been in a conversation where you say something but the other person changes subject or doesn't acknowledge your point of view? How did that make you feel? Were you annoyed or frustrated?

This annoyance has happened to all of us. The other person wasn't listening. But I want you to remember that feeling because when you don't listen to other people, you make them feel that way. By not listening, you're not respecting their point of view and you're being inconsiderate. You don't want to be that person. You're better than that.

Poor communication leads to broken and/or damaged relationships. Instead, you want to be considerate, respectful, and tactful by practicing effective communication habits.

Here are several effective communication habits you'll want to adopt if you want to be a great communicator and friend:

Actively Listen

Effective listeners actively listen to people by nodding their heads, using their faces to express emotion, and adding in reassuring language like, "I understand," "Wow, that's incredible!" and "Good for you!"

In other words, you want the other person to know you're truly listening by actively and genuinely responding to what she's saying.

Wait Your Turn

During a conversation, it's important to wait for the other person to acknowledge you before you begin speaking. It's insensitive and rude to jump right into your own monologue after the person finishes their thought. Listen... pause... and respond in a kind, considerate way that lets her know you were listening and not just thinking about what you wanted to say next. In addition, it's also impolite to talk over someone, take over a conversation, or finish the other person sentence.

Don't Talk Over Others

One of my biggest pet peeves is when people finish my sentences. I strongly believe that your thoughts are not my thoughts and vice versa. Letting someone talk without cutting her off shows respect and common courtesy. You can insert a comment, question, or concern when there is a pause in the conversation. Remember, conversing is like throwing a softball or baseball. You can only throw (offer) the ball (your thoughts and ideas) to the other person after you catch (hear) the ball (her thoughts and ideas) she throw to you.

Less Is More

When it's finally your turn to talk, keep in mind that "less is more." Meaning, a conversation is a dialogue and involves two or more people, so talking less can have more of an impact than talking more. Be clear and concise. Don't ramble on and on. And try to avoid talking about yourself too much. One way to help you with this is to think before you speak. Don't just blurt out what you want to say. Instead, think about what you want to say and communicate your thought as best you can. Then, once you're done making your point, let the other person jump in and add value to the conversation.

Speak Clearly and Correctly

People who don't know you will tend to judge you based on how you speak. So, take the time to make a great impression by speaking in a nice tone, using complete sentences, and clearly and correctly pronouncing every word. Not only will the other person enjoy the conversation more, the other person will understand you better and be able to show you the same respect you're showing her. In addition, do not chew gum when you are talking to someone. This may inhibit your ability to speak clearly.

Use Appreciation

Using words like "please" and "thank you" are not only kind but shows appreciation. After all, a person's time is the most precious asset she possesses. When someone gives you her time, she's giving you a piece of her life. Remember these tips next time you talk with other people, and be sure to always thank the other person for her time.

You Are Their First Teacher

Parenting isn't always easy. In fact, sometimes parenting can be a real challenge. But more often than not, parenting is the most rewarding job you'll ever have.

Currently, I am raising teenagers. And just like any good parent, I'm trying to raise them to be self-sufficient adults with the ability to make good, healthy, personal choices. But my attempts did not start recently. I started this trend when I brought those 'lil bundles of joy home from the hospital.

You see, children are born with over 100 billion brain cells that have very little neural connections. Think of a clean slate. Their neural connections are created by the words they hear, the actions everyone around them takes, and how their brain interrupts all the stimuli.

Meaning, your words and actions ultimately help shape their personality and character. So, if you teach and train your children now to be polite and kind, they'll be polite and kind as they grow up.

To assist you with this task, here are some helpful tips on good parenting and teaching your child manners:

Set Rules

If you do not manage your child's behavior when he or she is young, she will not know how to manage her behavior when she is older. This can interfere with your children's choices in school and have deeper consequences as they enter the workforce.

Be Consistent

Your "no" must mean NO. Saying what you mean and being consistent in your actions are critical. Your children are watching you and modeling your actions. In addition, your tone is very important when speaking to your child. You can convey the same message without hollering and nagging. Simply show her what "polite" looks like so she can see the kindness in your eyes. Remember, you are you child's first teacher.

Give Them a Role Model

I can't stress this enough, you must model the behavior that you want your children to emulate. You can't talk the talk and not walk the walk. When your child sees you being kind to someone, she will be kind too. When my children were younger, I spent a lot of time getting them to focus on using words like "Please," "May I," and "Thank you." Manners matter. And manners all start with your being a kind, considerate, respectful role model.

Understand Your Child Is Not You

This is a hard lesson, but you must learn to take the bad with the good. Your children are not you. Sometimes we lose sight of that, and we think they are supposed to think the way we do, act the way we do, and become what we want them to become. That's simply not the case. They are their own people. But they'll make better decisions and be self-sufficient when we show them what good manners look like, give them the freedom to be themselves, and give them the freedom make some mistakes.

Respect Your Child

You can't disrespect your children and require that they respect you. Have you ever heard the old-school parenting axiom, "Do as I say, not as I do?" While it's a catchy phrase, it's ignorant parenting advice. Respecting your child means to be considerate of her feelings, to listen, and to talk TO her not AT her. I understand. You won't always like her choices. But they are her choices, so meet her half way with love and respect. Look, I don't think you can ever love your child too much. Loving and respecting your children does not spoil them. Spoiling them becomes an issue when we try to replace love and respect with material things.

Don't Do THAT!

Do other people do things that annoy you? If you said "yes," you're not alone. A lot of us have pet peeves that drive us up the wall.

However, before you blame other people for their actions, consider this:

Do YOU do things that annoy other people?

If you're honest with yourself, then you can imagine that some of things you do on a regular basis may annoy or frustrate other people around you. Remember, those who live in glass houses, shouldn't throw stones.

So, let's take a look at some pet peeves that drive you and others crazy, so we can personally STOP DOING THEM, set the example for others to follow, and give ourselves and others a little peace of mind:

Being Late to Meet Someone

Whether you are intentionally or unintentionally

late for an appointment, an interview, a meeting, or just a get-together with a friend, you send a very clear message: I don't care about your time.

Remember, manners are about treating others with respect and courtesy. So, instead of running the risk of being late, plan ahead. If you're going somewhere you've never been before, look up the directions and know where you're going BEFORE you leave. Wake up early, leave early, and plan your time around traffic patterns. There really are no excuses for being late.

Now, if something does happen that is truly out of your control, then have good manners and make sure you give a courtesy phone call. That way the person knows you're on your way, AND she know that you respect their time.

Laying on Your Horn When Driving

Not everybody drives like you do, and it's important to realize that people make a mistakes on the road. However, laying on your horn to alert them that you are displeased is not going to fix the issue. Yes, there are times when you should give a friendly "beep" to alert another driver that you're behind her or that she should go when the light turns green. But giving a long, annoying H-O-O-O-N-K is never appropriate. That will only cause road rage in the culprit and annoy other drivers.

In addition, here are some other driving related pet peeves and/or illegal activities: parking in middle of street, not stopping for pedestrians in crosswalk, taking up two parking spaces, driving too close to another car (i.e. on someone's "rear end"), driving too slow, and driving too fast. Again, let's be kind and courteous to others while keeping us all safe!

Coughing, Sneezing, & Yawning Without Covering Your Mouth

Not only are these habits unsanitary, but they're also rude and inconsiderate. Listen, getting sick is no fun, and coughing or sneezing without covering your mouth is gross. So, we can all do each other a favor by covering our mouths and noses when we cough or sneeze. The same is true when you yawn. No one wants to see the inside of your mouth or be exposed to your germs.

Non-Stop Complaining

Talk about a BIG TURN OFF! No one likes to be around someone who is always complaining and never seeing the good in anything. A few years ago, I was at a restaurant with a friend, and she couldn't find anything complimentary to say about the place. She complained about the location. She complained about the food. She complained about the service. Sheesh! Her non-stop complaining really made me feel uncomfortable.

And I felt sorry for the waiter, who was catching the most grief. Listen, having standards and speaking up for what you want are both very good things. However, for the sake of those around you, sometimes it's just best to be calm and make a different decision next time.

Attention Seeking

Have you ever been around someone who always needs to be the center of attention? Sure, having the spotlight on you sometimes feels good, but letting someone else shine too is the only polite thing to do. For example, when someone is sharing a story about her child's graduation, allow her to shine and enjoy her moment. There's no need to take over the story and dampen her limelight. Let her be the center of attention. Remember, conversing is like playing baseball – you have to pitch AND catch!

Parents Letting Their Children Scream In The Presence Of Others

We've all been there. We've all experienced a child screaming at the top of his or her lungs. And there's nothing wrong with this. It's natural. However, letting your child scream in the presence of others for an extended period of time is rude and inconsiderate.

Now granted, calming an upset child can be challenging. But that doesn't mean you have to let the child continue screaming. For example, if you're in a closed space, removing yourself and your child from the situation can relieve the anxiety of your child and other people. If you are at a friend's home, sometimes it's best to suggest leaving. If the screaming really doesn't bother your friend, he or she will ask you to stay.

Constantly Making Negative Comments

I'm sure you've heard the saying, "One bad apple can spoil the whole bunch." Negative people are like that bad apple. They are toxic, and they have a way of INFECTNG others and spoiling a perfectly good event or conversation. Staying positive and associating yourself with positive people is always better. People who see the glass half full are always more fun to be around. Look, good manners are not just about your actions, having good manners is also about your attitude. Stay positive, and learn to have a great attitude toward people and life.

Refusing a Compliment

I think it's human nature to sometimes see ourselves in a negative light. However, for our own sake, learning to compliment ourselves and accept compliments from others is crucial. Let me ask you a question. Has a friend ever said, "I like your hair cut," only for you to retort like, "My hair looks a mess, I'm actually getting it done tomorrow?" I don't know about you, but I've been there before. However, what you may or may not realize is that you have just insulted the person giving you the compliment. Instead, a simple "thank you" is all it takes to receive the compliment and make the other person feel good.

Chewing With Your Mouth Open

No one wants to see mashed, slobber-covered, slightly-digested food sloshing around in your mouth. In most instances, food should be chewed with your mouth closed. On rare occasions, when you must talk with food in your mouth (e.g. at a business dinner) you can put your hand in front of your mouth to shield your food and continue your conversation. Eating small bites can help in these situations and prevent you from showing people more than they bargained for. In addition, chewing gum while speaking with someone is not polite either.

Speak Up and Say Something

Have you ever been in a situation where someone enters the room and doesn't say a word? It's awkward, isn't it? What is she doing? What is she thinking? Is she your friend or your enemy?

This type of behavior is unsettling for most people. And since our goal is to always make sure we're setting people's minds at ease and making them feel comfortable, a simple rule to live by is: the person who enters the room first should speak first.

So, no matter who you meet or see today – whether it's your husband, your children, a friend, a coworker, or a complete stranger - show good manners and common courtesy by speaking first.

You become more pleasant to be around when you are kind and when you greet someone with a friendly gesture of "Good morning" or "Hello." Manners come from within. Being polite, kind, and considerate is all about character. Your personality is how people see you. Your character is how you see yourself - who you are within.

When you greet someone for the first time, show her who you really are by smiling and giving her a warm "good morning," "good afternoon," or "good evening."

When it comes to speaking, here are some additional courtesies that you should incorporate in your daily routine:

Say "Please" and "Thank You" Often

Learning to say these words will soften any situation and show people that you respect their time, their energy, and their worth.

Be Helpful

When you see a need to lend a helping hand, assist your friend or fellow human being! For example, if you're visiting a friend's home and she starts setting the table, speak up and ask if she needs any help.

If you're at the grocery store and see an elderly gentleman who needs assistance, speak up and ask if he needs help.

Respect Others' Opinions

It's a fact. Everyone has her own opinion. By the way, that's a good thing. How boring would the world be if everyone thought the same? Pretty boring and mundane, wouldn't you say? If someone shares a belief, value, or opinion that is different from yours, accept the difference, and keep the conversation moving. You don't have to agree with the other person. The key is to respect her opinion just as you would want someone to respect yours.

Don't Assume It's About You

Sometimes people have a bad day. The worst thing you can do is assume that their mood is about you. In fact, it's important to realize that you should never assume anything if you want to know something. Simply ask in a respectful tone, and you'll find out what's really going on. Only then can you lend a helping hand or a listening ear.

Oops! I Hope I Didn't Say the Wrong Thing

Have you ever found yourself in a sticky situation and you didn't know if what you were saying was appropriate or not?

People who have good manners are always cautious about saying the right thing. So much so that they will spare themselves the embarrassment by saying nothing at all.

As I mentioned earlier, being a good listener is sometimes all you need to do. When you are being polite and practicing good manners, you should always put others at ease and make everyone around you feel comfortable. Here are some topics that make people feel uncomfortable to talk about because they don't know what to say:

Bad Hygiene

Have you ever spoken with someone who's body

or oral hygiene was lacking? If so, I'm sure you felt pretty uncomfortable, especially if you were in a shared space. Do you say something about the odor or try to ignore it? Do you offer them a mint or put your hand over your nose?

The short answer is this: don't embarrass or make others uncomfortable – even though their hygiene is making you uncomfortable.

For example, if you're reaching for a mint, then offering them a mint is polite. However, you should never offer anyone a mint out of the blue. That's too direct and can embarrass the other person.

You should never tell someone about her poor hygiene, especially if you don't have a relationship with her. And even if you do have a relationship with the offender, you should tread lightly. The situation is too touchy. No matter what you say, you'll come across as rude and crude. It is never polite to hurt someone's feelings, even if you think you are helping her.

Now, on the other hand, if the person's bad hygiene frequently occurs in the workplace or at school, you should discuss the situation with your superior and let her handle it. You don't want to be impolite, but you shouldn't have to suffer in silence either.

Losing a Loved One

This topic should always be handled with care. Never tell someone that her loved one is in a better place or "at least your loved one isn't suffering any longer." That's your opinion and the bereaving person may not feel the same way. She may want her loved one here with her regardless of the circumstance.

This situation is when graciousness needs to step in. Try to support the other person without being too intrusive and overbearing.

The most famous line we say to others after they lose someone is, "Call me if you need anything." Yes, you have good intentions. But have you ever lost anyone? Your mind is not on calling anyone, even if there is a need. Your mind is elsewhere. You're grieving, and you're not in the frame of mind to talk to anyone.

Instead, I've found that waiting to offer your help is best. Try to be considerate and try to see the situation from the other person's point of view. The person is grieving, and she doesn't know what she needs or what will help. I have found that sending a card with the simple phrase, "You are in my thoughts, and I will check on you and your family at a later time," is sufficient and much appreciated.

Lastly, family members of the deceased typically find more comfort when support is rendered after everything is over. Allow them space and time. Then, when all the traffic calms down and all the out-of-town guests are gone, offer to visit and/or assist with food. This is when the support is really needed. Keep that in mind!

Attending a Funeral

No one enjoys going to a funeral. However, it's not about you. Funerals are about the ones who are grieving. Your presence goes a long way. When someone is in a time of need, just being there for her may give her the support she needs.

In addition, when you attend the funeral service, keep in mind that the grieving person is not responsible for keeping you company. Politely offer a hug or a handshake, whichever you feel most appropriate, then keep the receiving line moving. Trying to hold a long conversation is awkward and impolite – and completely exhausting for the people who are grieving.

Bringing something to offer the grieving person is unnecessary. However, if you do plan on bringing something and you are not sure what to bring, bottled water is always a good idea. And if you know what the family needs, try to support them the best way you can. You don't have to go beyond your limits. The family will be grateful for whatever you bring.

Divorce or Separation

Adjusting to a new life can be a little difficult, so showing good manners and being polite means knowing when to offer an opinion and when to just lend an empathetic ear. After all, you don't know the thoughts and emotions the other person is experiencing. She may want the other person back. Or she may want to move on with her life. Listen and respond with empathy.

In addition, regardless of what happened with the situation, do not tell the newly divorced or separated that they are better off without the other person. While you may have good intentions or you're trying to cheer up your friend, that statement is crass and shows a lack of empathy. Plus, how do you think she'll feel about you if she gets back together with her spouse? Keeping those types of opinions to yourself is best.

Lastly, do not take it personally if the person going through the divorce or separation needs some time to herself to sort things out. She may even seem a little distant. That's okay. Transitioning is hard for some people, so allow them time and respect their space.

Losing a Job

If a friend or colleague is laid off or fired, give her the time and space she needs to process the situation. Being laid off or fired can be traumatic event for some people. And the last thing they want to hear when they feel like their world is crumbling in front of them is, "You'll be okay." Unsolicited advice is your opinion. Allow people time to figure things out for themselves. Again, never take things personally when people are trying to sort out big things like this.

Now, one thing you can say to show your support is, "I'm here if you need me." We all need someone, so letting your friend or colleague know that you're there for her is sometimes all the support she needs.

Lastly, never get caught up in rumors or gossip, especially if you still work at the same place your friend or colleague was laid off or fired from. Participating in rumors or gossip is not only discourteous, speaking about people behind their backs can also get you into a sticky situation down the road.

Expecting or Not Expecting, That Is the Question?

Pregnancy can be a very touchy subject. So, first things first: if you don't know for sure (as in the person told you), don't assume or guess that someone is pregnant! Doing so can make you look foolish and embarrass the other person. Typically, women like to share this kind of news in their own time, so there is really no need for you to ask. When she is ready to tell you, she'll tell you.

Second, for couples who are married and do not have children, asking them when or if they will start a family is impolite. Again, people share what they want you to know. This topic may seem like light conversation to you; however, if there is a medical problem or a circumstance that prevents them from conceiving, you'll put yourself in an awkward position and make the other party feel uncomfortable by bringing it up.

Remember, having good manners is all about treating people with respect and kindness, while not embarrassing them or making them feel uneasy. Motherhood is a wonderful thing. But to some people, motherhood or parenting may not be a priority. So, never pass judgment or assume. And don't make anyone feel bad for the choices she or he have made to consciously wait or refrain from having children.

Visiting the Sick

When someone is sick, showing your support by paying her a visit is always a nice gesture. However, while you may love to surprise people by showing up unexpectedly, I don't advise surprising anyone who's sick. By doing so, you may show up at an inopportune time. The person may be resting, eating, having testing done, or visiting with her doctor (if she's in the hospital). Now, the one way to get around this is by making sure that it's an appropriate time to visit. For example, you can call her house or hospital room and speak to a family member to make sure it's a good time. You can also call the nurses station to see if it's a good time to visit.

Also, when someone is sick, the one thing he or she needs most is rest! So if the person is in the hospital, stay up to 20 minutes but no longer. And if her doctor walks in to see her, be respectful, give your friend privacy, and step out the room until the doctor is finished. If the person is at home, understand that entertaining you is not what she needs. Don't overstay your welcome. Stay for up to 20 minutes, then leave and allow her to rest.

Should you bring something when visiting the sick? Yes. But I don't recommend flowers because the patient may be allergic to flowers. Instead, a simple card with your kindly written words inside is sufficient. Or if your friend likes to read, bringing her a book is a nice, inexpensive option.

Don't Invade Someone's Personal Boundaries

Each and every one of us has personal boundaries. Some of these boundaries are physical, while other boundaries are mental and emotional.

For example, when you stand within someone's personal space (i.e. standing within three feet of the person), you're intruding on her physical boundary. This makes most people feel uncomfortable and defensive.

Now, there are exceptions. When you date someone, you're allowed to stand or move inside his physical boundary. He's given you permission because he trusts you, and he wants you close to him. However, unless you're intimate with someone, standing at a safe distance (three to six feet away) is courteous and respectful.

Other boundaries have a mental and emotional component to them. For example, have you ever been in a situation where one person attempts to completely take over a conversation and steamrolls over everyone else trying to talk?

It's uncomfortable, isn't it? Sure, you don't necessarily feel the same as when someone invades your personal space, but you do feel violated and unappreciated. After all, you're important, and you have important things to say and contribute to the conversation.

So, to help you respect others' personal boundaries, here are a few things to avoid doing in a conversation:

Physical Boundaries

- Don't stand inside someone's personal space. It's best to stand or sit three to six feet away from someone. Any closer will make most people feel uncomfortable.

- Don't touch people unless they're friends or loved ones. Yes, it's natural to shake a stranger's hand when you first meet her; however, other types of touching are typically inappropriate. For instance, hugging someone you don't know or trust could break her physical boundary and make her feel uncomfortable.

Mental/Emotional Boundaries

- Don't be pushy or overbearing. You're not the only person in the conversation. Respect what others have to say and realize that it's not just about you.

- Don't say everything that comes into your head. Some things are better left unsaid, and not everything said or done requires a response. Listen and respond if necessary.

- Tread lightly when asking personal questions. Asking someone about her finances, relationships, or family can sometimes cross over her emotional boundary and be looked at as disrespectful. Tread lightly and don't push people beyond their current limits.

People with a Disability Want to Be Treated Like Everyone Else

There are more than 50 million Americans who suffer from a disability. Some disabilities are vision related and others include hearing, speech, and mobility impairments.

Unless you have experience interacting with people with a disability, you may feel a little uncomfortable when you have the opportunity for that kind of interaction. That's okay to admit. However, it's important to understand that being kind, polite, and showing good manners – no matter who you're dealing with – is always welcomed.

And while this is sometimes a touchy subject to talk about, you must learn how to interact with someone with a disability. So, the first thing you must realize is this: in most cases, **people with a disability want to be treated like everyone else**.

So, to help you feel more comfortable when interacting with a person with a disability (as well as to make her or him feel comfortable and respected), here are a few tips on interacting with anyone with a disability:

- Don't label. Many people with disabilities are in perfectly good health.
- Don't ask directly what anyone's disability is. Allow people to tell you what they want you to know.
- Don't use words like "handicapped" or "crippled." The more respectful and polite word is "disabled."
- You can acknowledge the disability but place the person first. You're not talking to a disabled person. You're talking to a person with a disability. The distinction is subtle but very important.
- Offering to assist someone is never an impolite thing to do. But if the person declines your assistance, don't insist to help her just because it makes you feel better. Let her accept or decline your help, and respect her decision no matter what the verdict.

- Despite what you have been taught or understand about anyone with a disability, don't assume anything. Not everyone with a disability will look or act the same.

Respect Your Elders

I recently visited a senior home facility, and I asked a group of seniors, "What tends to annoy you as you get older and wiser?"

Can you guess what they told me their number one frustration is? It's when people get impatient with them.

I was intrigued by that answer, so I continued to ask questions. From the seniors' perspective, people grow impatient with them when they cannot complete a simple task correctly or when they cannot complete a task in a timely manner.

Listen, I completely appreciate the fact that impatience is a natural human emotion, and we will all feel impatient at some point. However, we will all go through the aging process at some point; and when we do, our bodies and minds will start to slow down too.

We will no longer be able to think as quickly as we used to. We will not be able to move as swiftly as we used to. We will no longer be as graceful as we are today. And we will experience a decrease in our reaction time. These are all a facts of life.

So, with that knowledge in mind, let me ask you a question: how would you feel if people constantly got impatient with you? You wouldn't like it, would you? Me neither.

How would you feel if someone was impatient and disrespectful to your mother or grandmother? Again, you wouldn't like it. Nobody would.

So, let's keep this in mind when we're interacting with our elders. They've lived a long life. They deserve our courtesy and kindness. And they deserve our respect.

How to Stay Friends Forever

Someone once told me, "Friends are God's way of taking care of us. They are our personal angels sent from heaven."

I believe that saying to be true. And because I feel that your friends were put into your life to take care of you, I also believe you must always be mindful, kind, and polite to your personal angels.

Here are a few things to keep in mind, so you can stay friends forever:

It's Not About You

When your friends are having a bad day, don't continuously ask them, "What's wrong?"

I know it's a natural thing to ask, but there may be nothing wrong. In that case, your concern can get annoying if you're constantly asking them.

On the other hand, something may be wrong, but they just aren't ready to talk about it. In that case, your concern can aggravate them and intensify their negative emotions.

Again, I understand that you're concerned for your friend. But you have to understand that her mood is not about you. Her emotions are about her. When she's ready to tell you something, she'll come to you. That's what friends do.

So instead, you can be a good friend by saying something like this: "I see you are not your usual self. If or when you want to chat, I'm here." Then, walk away.

This allows your friend to digest what's on her mind, while showing her you care and that you're there for her.

Don't Stick Your Nose Where It Doesn't Belong

No one enjoys receiving unsolicited advice or opinions, so don't succumb to the urge of giving unsolicited advice or opinions. Doing so will do nothing but put strain on your friendship.

If there is a disagreement between friends that does not involve you, DO NOT INVOLVE YOUR-

SELF. Stay neutral, and do not form an opinion until you have heard both sides.

Then, when you're asked for your opinion, tactfully share your opinion in a way that shows you care but doesn't tell anyone what to do or take sides. Remember, being a good friend is all about having trust and being non-judgmental.

NOTE: Everything in this chapter applies to your family as well, especially this tip. Whatever you do, do not stick your nose in other friends' or family members' business. It's rude and impolite.

Choose Your Battles

Sometimes you and your friends will not agree on things. That's okay. In fact, that's natural. We all have our own opinions, and we all have our own view points. However, the key to disagreements in any relationship is to know how to choose your battles.

Fighting about everything little thing will end a friendship in a blink of an eye. Choose the battles you're willing to fight for and politely forfeit the rest. Now, I'm not talking about giving up your point of view. Instead, be smart and graciously let the other person have her opinion while you have your own.

Some call this arrangement "agreeing to disagree." Others call it "learning to let go." Whatever you call it, understanding and exercising this principle will surely bring you peace and happiness. If you value the relationship, you must learn to let some things go.

Don't Be a Gossip

Webster's defines a gossip as "a person who habitually reveals personal or sensational facts about others." Friendships are built on trust, and one of the quickest ways to break someone's trust to gossip or spread rumors about her.

Look, your friends tell you things because they have trust and confidence in you. Talking behind their backs is not only rude, it can be psychologically devastating to people who don't easily open up to others.

We spend years developing and shaping our character and identity. Gossip, rumors, and untruths can unintentionally rip someone's character and identity apart in a matter of days.

In addition, if you are engaging in a conversation with someone who says, "This is between you and me," chances are she's a gossip, and you shouldn't let her mouth accidentally ruin your relationships and friendships with others.

An Apology Goes a Long Way

We all have bad days. But just because you are having a bad day doesn't give you the right to treat your friends (or anyone else for that matter) in a rude or disrespectful manner.

Life is full of mistakes. Sometimes you'll make a mistake and be in the wrong. Other times, your friends will make a mistake and you'll feel hurt. There are two very important life lessons to learn from this.

First, if you've offended a friend, saying the words, "I'm sorry," can change the dynamic and the outcome of the situation. Yes, sometimes justifying a situation feels good. But that's a short-sighted attitude. You're in this friendship for the long-haul, so be the bigger person and apologize for your actions.

An apology goes a long way, and saying you're sorry speaks volumes about your character and the value you place on the relationship.

A while back I read the following quote on apologizing: "When you value your relationships, learn to be apologetic because it's not always about who's right or wrong, it's about valuing the relationship more than your ego." That quote has made an impact on my life. I hope it impacts your life too.

Second, when you are the one who's offended, you have the right to be upset, hurt, frustrated, and disappointed. However, realize that whatever happened, HAPPENED – it's in the past – and you can't undo it.

All you can do is talk about the situation, hopefully hear an apology from your friend, forgive her for the mistake she's (more likely than not) accidentally made, and move on.

Yes, your friends will get on your nerves from time to time, but remember that valued and healthy relationships are worth preserving.

Be A Gracious Guest

A couple years ago, a friend of mine purchased a new house and invited me and a few friends over for a small get together. When we arrived, she asked us to please remove our shoes. A simple request, right? I thought so too, so I removed my shoes and made my way into her new, beautiful home.

However, for some reason, one of our friends took offense to the request and made a fuss about it. She didn't feel the need to take off her shoes, and she was upset that our hostess even asked.

Have you ever heard the cliché, "When in Rome, do as the Romans do?" Abiding by the customs of a society or culture where you are a visitor is not only polite but possibly advantageous. For example, when you're in Rome, it's polite and advantageous to abide by their customs and rules.

The same goes for when you're in someone else's home. Being a gracious guest means that you know how to comply with the homeowner's rules.

Here are a few other tips to aid you in being a gracious house guest:

Be Early, But Not Too Early

I believe you should always be early to where you're going. However, if you're visiting someone's home, being too early is impolite. So, a good rule of thumb is to arrive at someone's home no more than 10 minutes early. That way they can prepare for you and the other guests without feeling rushed or anxious.

Some Simple Do's & Don'ts

To avoid awkwardness, here are a handful of simple do's and don'ts to adhere to when being a guest:

- Always call before you make an unexpected visit.

- Don't overstay your welcome.

- Always bring a small gift (i.e. flowers, wine, chocolates).

- Don't show up with an unexpected guest.

- Always be modest in the amount of food you eat.

- Don't eat a second helping while guests are still coming in or on their way.

- Always tell the host ahead of time if you are allergic to something.

- Don't open closed doors or roam around without permission.

- Always treat the host's guests with kindness and respect.

- Don't make negative comments about what food has been prepared.

- Always offer to help clean up.

- Don't smoke inside the house without permission.

When You Disagree With Their Rules

Now, there may be times when you don't agree with someone's rules or customs. That's okay. You're allowed your own opinions. However, breaking the host's or hostess' rules is rude. And that's not okay. Remember, manners are about treating others with respect and courtesy.

If for some reason you don't agree with their rules, either keep your opinion to yourself or leave. There's no point in getting angry or bitter over the matter. Their rules are their rules. And if you choose to stay and decide afterwards that their rules bother you too much, you don't have to visit them again.

High Touch Always Beats High Tech

In today's technology-driven world, we all use smart phones, email, and social media to communicate with each other. However, it's important to realize that technology provides us with tools to communicate more easily, and technology does not replace the power of actual human interaction.

Yes, being connected with your family and friends is great, but being considerate to others while using your technology is just as important. So, here are some simple tips to help you communicate better without annoying or rudely distracting others:

Be Mindful of Others

When you are in public, turning off your cell phone or putting it on vibrate is a good rule of thumb. It's rude to subject other people to your loud and/or obnoxious ring tones and notifications.

Also, when you must take a phone call in public, excuse yourself and find somewhere quiet and away from others to talk. Just like your ring tones and notifications, forcing your conversation on those around you is discourteous, especially if they're in the movie theater, concert, or any other dark, public location.

In addition, be mindful of those around you when you're taking selfies and pictures with friends. This is especially true when you're posting your pictures on social media sites without the other person's consent.

Relationships Are the Goal

More likely than not, you use technology as a tool to stay connected and further develop your relationships with your family and friends. So if that's the case, then don't let your cell phone or digital device take precedent over the person with whom you're talking. If you're talking with someone, look at her and not your phone. When you're meeting someone for coffee or lunch, be present and not swept up in a virtual conversation with someone who is dozens or hundreds of miles away.

If you absolutely *must* take a call or answer a text (and that should be a rare occurrence), then ask her if she minds you taking the call or answering the text. Nine out of ten times the person will not mind at all because you gave her the respect she deserves.

Sidestep These Texting Taboos

In my opinion, texting is one of the greatest inventions of our time. Think about it. Texting allows you to instantly communicate with your family and friends no matter where you are. And texting communicates in a non-threatening, non-time-intensive manner. Brilliant! Now, with that said, there are some texting taboos you'll want to avoid.

First, when you're texting someone for the first time or someone you rarely text, be sure to state who you are, avoid the use of acronyms (they may confuse the other person), and keep your texts short and to the point (for goodness sake call them if the conversion is getting too long).

Second, it's inconsiderate and cruel to leave bad news via text, especially when the news is about break-ups and deaths. Don't do that, that's awful.

Third, limit the number of texts you send because your friends may not have unlimited texting and you could run up their bill. And when you send a group text, if your answer only involves one person, send your answer to only that person and not the entire group.

Fourth, be patient with others when you're waiting for a reply. Texting is meant to be done when the time permits, not when you want an answer to arrive. If you want an answer quickly, call the person or go see her.

Last, NEVER EVER text and drive! Texting is not worth your life – or someone else's life. Texting can wait!

Become Social Media Savvy

Social media sites, like Facebook, Instagram, Snapchat, Twitter, LinkedIn, etc. can be used to entertain you, keep you connected to family and friends, or be a resource for your career.

However, since anything you post can be retrieved (even if you delete it), becoming social media savvy is very important so you don't get burnt in the long run. Here are some quick tips to help you:

- Do not put confidential information on your personal or business sites. Doing so can set you up to have your identity or your banking information stolen.

- Customize your privacy settings so only certain people will be privy to information on your page. Letting everyone see your feed and profile can open you up to too many negative situations.

- There is no reason you have to be tagged in all photos. Keeping some anonymity is a good thing.

- Just because someone is following you doesn't necessarily mean you must follow her.

- Never use social media to air out dirty laundry. If you have an issue with someone, then pick up the phone or go see her. Resolve your issue and clear the air offline, not online.

- Never misrepresent yourself in any way. You never know who's looking at your information and what any exaggerations or tall tales can do to your future.

- Be careful of what you say. Offensive language can not only get you banned from sites, it can also offend people you may want to get to know in the future (i.e. a future boss or a college recruiter). That rule also goes for jokes and humor. Just because you post something you think is funny, your positive reaction doesn't mean other's will feel the same way. Never post things that are offensive or that could be misinterpreted as inappropriate. (With that being said, if you are using social media sites for entertainment purposes, please don't use your government name. Remember, everything you post is PERMANENT! If you don't want someone – like a future boss or college administrator – to see your social media posts, then keep your name off your sites.)

Avoid Simple Phone Faux Pas

When I was younger, the phone was our landline to the outside world (pun intended). Nowadays, the phone "feature" on our smart phones is used less than any other feature. That's why understanding how to avoid a couple phone faux pas when you do use the phone feature is so important. For instance, when you call someone, be courteous and ask the person you're calling if it's a good time to talk. If you're leaving a voice message, then be clear and professional with your name, number, and reason for calling.

Last, if your voice message states that you will return the call… then return the call! Your word is your bond, so do what you say you'll do.

The Bare Essentials to Dining Out

Years ago, most manners were taught around the table. However, in the typical American family both parents are now working long hours (even sometimes working even after they get home), and sitting around the table to eat is a thing of the past.

Yes, many families still get together for those holiday dinners and occasional Sunday meals, but most of the time, they are grabbing food and eating on the go.

So, in case you were never taught proper table manners and etiquette (or you just want to brush up), here are the bare essentials to understand when dining out with others (your family included):

Never Openly Make Negative Comments About the Food

If you are not pleased with your meal, simply get

the waiter and discretely tell her about your issue. Don't say things like "the food is nasty" or "this meal is gross." Instead, say "this meal is not to my liking, can you bring me _____?" Calling a restaurant's food "gross" or "nasty" is disrespectful.

Discreetly asking them to bring you something else is not only polite, it's in good taste (no pun intended). To avoid this mishap, try to order food that you are familiar with. That way you won't run the risk of having to send food back.

Forks, Knives, and Spoons, Oh My!

Forks and napkin on left only. Spoons, knives, and glasses on the right. The place setting is important to know this because if you are sitting at a round table and you grab the wrong glass or fork, you will mess up the whole rotation of the table.

Remembering where to place your silverware is easy if you remember the following trick: you spell "left," "fork," and "wipe" (as in you wipe your mouth with your napkin) with 4 letters, and you spell "right," "glass," "spoon," and "knife" with 5 letters. See this little trick visually on the next page...

LEFT	**RIGHT**
FORK	GLASS
WIPE	SPOON
	KNIFE

In addition, never pick up silverware that fell on the floor and put it back on the table. Anything soiled should never go on the table. Instead, leave the dirtied utensil on the floor! Yes, I know this sounds counter-intuitive, but you are supposed to leave the utensil on the floor and inform the waiter. She will bring you another set.

Paying a Group Bill

When you're dining in a group, the best method for dividing the bill is to divide by the number in the party. When you have a party of four or more and you start itemizing the bill, it's cumbersome and embarrassing. To make things fair, you may consider putting alcohol on a separate bill for those who do not drink alcohol. If you must itemize the bill, for whatever reason, politely inform the waiter beforehand.

Tip Your Waiter

Waiters and waitresses live off their tips, so rewarding them when they do a good job is important. How much should you tip your waiter or waitress? A good rule of thumb is based on his or her service, with the minimum percentage I suggest being 15%. So, if you really didn't enjoy the service, then only tip the minimum required 15%. If the staff provided mediocre service, then tipping them 18-20% is sufficient. And if they provided stellar service, I've tipped my wait staff as much as 25%.

Decide on Your Order, Then Talk

If you're like me, then you love talking to your friends and loved ones when you go out to eat. However, looking over the menu and deciding on your order before you get too caught up in conversation is the courteous thing to do for your waiter or waitress.

Remember, your wait staff gets paid based on the tips they collect. So, the more tables they're able to service, the more money they're able to make. Yes, dining out is a pleasure you should enjoy immensely. But wasting the waiters' time and livelihood is inconsiderate. Order your food first, and then talk to your heart's content.

Unruly Kids

Exposing children to fine dining is a beautiful thing, but not if they are being unruly and messing up someone else's dining experience. If your child is disgruntled, try your best to calm him or her down. If that doesn't work, then leave the dining area and go to the hallway or vestibule area until she calms down. Remember, you're not the only one dining out. Respect other people's dining experience.

Pace Yourself

Try to pace yourself with everyone at the table. In other words, do not eat too fast or too slow. Instead, pace yourself, so you're done eating around the same time as everyone else. Finishing before everyone else can make them feel rushed. Finishing after everyone can make your table guests anxious and uncomfortable.

Some Miscellaneous Rules

Here are a handful of miscellaneous rules to follow when eating out:

- Always wait until everyone is served before you start eating.

- Never tell people at the table why you need to be excused. If you need to be excused from the table, you simply say, "Excuse me." Spare them the details.

- Always use the words "please" and "thank you."

- Don't put your cell phone on the table or use your cell phone at the table. Dining out is all about good food and great conversation with the people you are with.

- Never use your personal utensils to dish out family-style food dishes. Use the utensils provided, so people don't have to second guess your spoon having your DNA on it.

- Don't double dip (dip, take a bite, then dip again with the same food). Other people don't want your germs for dinner.

- Never stare at others while they eat. It's creeping and impolite.

- Always respect others by chewing quietly, keeping your burps to yourself, and refraining from talking too loud or with food in your mouth.

- Never wipe your mouth and put the opened napkin on the table. That's just gross!

- Always place your napkin on your lap. If you're at an establishment with cloth napkins, placing your closed napkin on the table after you're finished eating is okay. However, if you're at an establishment with paper napkin, then keeping the napkin in your lap and throwing it away after you're finished eating is best practice.

Your Next Steps...

Congratulations on making it to the end of this book! I hope you found the tips and ideas inside to be both beneficial and enlightening. My hope is that you found yourself experiencing some "ah-ha moments" and maybe even saying to yourself, "Hmm... I never thought of that" or "I may need to work on that."

I encourage you to start with yourself and make the necessary changes to your behaviors that you feel will benefit your life and your future. I also encourage you not to place this book on a shelf to gather dust.

Instead, keep this book handy and use this book as a resource to help you navigate through life's uncomfortable situations.

If a thought like "I know someone who does that" crossed your mind while reading this book, then let me suggest picking up a copy for your friend. Yes, you could point out her flaws, but I don't recommend that.

Alternatively, let this book do the work for you without embarrassing your friend. I guarantee she'll thank you for believing in her and helping her change her attitude, her behaviors, and her life.

Maya Angelou said it best: "I've learned that people will forget what you said, people will forget what you did, but people will never forget how you made them feel." Use this book to make people feel respected and appreciated and to make them feel at ease in any situation.

Enjoy the book and be kind and courteous to others. I wish you all the best in your future endeavors!

~Sonya Chapman

About the Author

Sonya Chapman is a certified etiquette consultant and received her certification through the Charleston School of Protocol and Etiquette in South Carolina. She also holds a Master's Degree in Education.

While working in the education field, Sonya discovered her strong passion to shape students' and professionals' lives by teaching them the necessary social skills to be the best they could be and get what they desired in life.

In addition, Sonya is the founder of Chicago Protocol and Etiquette Consulting, Inc. – a Chicago-based consulting business that teaches individuals to empower themselves by refining and enhancing their social skills. Sonya is also a coach and speaker.

Sonya enjoys reading, shopping, networking, and spending time with her family. Sonya is married and has two children.

Book Sonya Chapman For Your Next Event!

Are you looking for a speaker who naturally connects with your audience?

Are you looking for a speaker who is enlightening, energetic, and can move your audience to action?

Are you looking for a speaker who brings a smile to everyone's face and leaves your audience wanting more?

If you answered "YES" to any of the above questions, then look no further. Sonya has trained adults and children from all walks of life, and she has spoken at schools, organizations, and companies on various topics including:

- Manners in America Are Dead
- Leadership In The 21st Century
- Ethics vs. Etiquette

- Enhancing Your Social Skills
- Prim And Proper Manners

If you are looking for a professional, experienced speaker, who can also make you laugh with her refreshingly transparent and effervescent personality, then call 773-412-0042 today to inquire about hiring Sonya Chapman for your next event. You can also reach Sonya via email at Sonya@cpecinc.com or by visiting: EtiquetteWithSonya.com.

Made in the USA
Middletown, DE
10 February 2019